MORPHOLOGY CHARTS

These pages contain blank charts of all the atypical verb-, noun- and adjective-types; of the four most important -μι verbs; and of sixty-four verbs with difficult, or atypical, principal parts. These charts should be filled in by the student under the teacher's guidance as the Course progresses.

Notes

1. Superior numbers indicate the section of the *Text* (*not* of the *Grammar*) after which particular forms should be filled in.

2. All stems have been given, so that **only endings should be filled in.** If you can fill in the whole word without impossible cramping and lack of clarity, do: but in most cases there will only be room for the ending anyway.

3. Sheets 1 and 2 should be taped together for use as one page.

T0349550

				FEMININE			
				singular			
c.[1]	gen.[7]	dat.[8]		nom.[2]	acc.[2]	gen.[7]	dat.[8]
			def. art.				
			1a noun βο-ή				
			καλ-ή				
			ἡμετέρ-α				
			1b noun ἀπορί-α				
			1c noun τόλμ-α				
				MASCULINE			
			1d noun ναύτ-ης				
			νεανί-ας				

		FEMININE			
		singular			
	dat.[8]	nom.[3]	acc.[3]	gen.[7]	dat.[8]
		μεγαλ-			
		πολλ-			
	τουτ-	αὐτ-	ταυτ-	ταυτ-	ταυτ-

VES

SITIVE	COMPARATIVE	SUPERLATIVE
ιθ-ός[6]		
[7]		
χρ-ός		
λ-ός[6]		
ς-ός[6]		
ϝας[7]		
γ-ος		
ιύς[6]		
ῥι-ος		

plural			
nom.[1]	acc.[1]	gen.[7]	dat.[8]

...en.[7]	dat.[8]	plural			
		nom.[3]	acc.[3]	gen.[7]	dat.[8]
εγαλ-		μεγαλ-			
ολλ-		πολλ-			
ουτ-	τουτ-	ταυτ-	ταυτ-	τουτ-	τουτ-

NOUNS AND ADJECTIVES – THIRD DECLENSION

singular		nom.	stem		acc.	gen.⁷	dat.⁸	plural nom.	acc.	gen.⁷	dat.⁸ *
noun 3a	m./f.	λιμήν	(λιμεν-)	3							
adjective	m./f.	εὔφρων**	(εὐφρον-)	4							
τίς/τις	m./f.	τίς	(τιν-)	4							
τί/τι	n.	τί	(τιν-)	4							
adjective	n.	εὔφρον**	(εὐφρον-)	4							
noun 3b	n.	πρᾶγμα	(πραγματ-)	4							
noun 3h	m./f.	ὀφρῦς	(ὀφρυ-)	5							

* where the stem ends in a single consonant, it is either removed or coalesces (e.g. λιμήν stem λιμεν- dat. pl. λιμέ-σι, but φύλαξ stem φυλακ-, dat. pl. φύλα-ξι)

** Comparative εὐφρον-έστερ-ος   Superlative εὐφρον-έστατ-ος

singular		nom.	stem		acc.	gen.⁷	dat.⁸	plural nom.	acc.	gen.⁷	dat.⁸
noun 3c	n.	πλῆθος	(πληθ-(ε)-)	4							
adjective	n.	ἀμελές**	(ἀμελ-(ε)-)	9							
adjective	m./f.	ἀμελής**	(ἀμελ-(ε)-)	9							
noun 3d	m./f.	Σωκράτης	(Σωκρατ-(ε)-)	5							
	m./f.	τριήρης	(τριηρ-(ε)-)	5							

* insert -ε- from stem

** Comparative ἀμελ-έστερ-ος   Superlative ἀμελ-έστατ-ος

singular		nom.	stem		acc.	gen.⁷	dat.⁸	plural nom.	acc.	gen.⁷	dat.⁸
noun 3e	f.	πόλις	(πολ-)	4							

ACTIVE παύ-ω 'I stop' (with strong aorist of λαμβάν-ω)

	1. PRESENT		2.FUTURE	3. AORIST		4. PERFECT	
a. INDICATIVE (TEMPORAL)							
	Present[1]	Imperfect[5]	Future[5]	Weak[5]	Strong[5]	Perfect[12]	Pluperfect[15]
	'I stop'	'I was -ing'	'I shall -'	'I stopped'	'I took'	'I have -ed'	'I had -ed'
1st s.	παυ-	ἐ-παυ-	παυσ-	ἐ-παυσ-	ἐ-λαβ-	πε-παυκ-	ἐ-πε-παυκ-
2nd s.							
3rd s.							
1st pl.							
2nd pl.							
3rd pl.							
b. UNAUGMENTED FORMS (ASPECTUAL)							
	Imperative[1/8]		Imperative	Imperative[8]	Imperative[8]	Impérative*	
2nd s.	παυ-		N	παυσ-	λαβ-	πέ-παυκ-ε	
3rd s.			O			-ετω	
2nd pl.			N			-ετε	
3rd pl.			E			-ετωσαν	
	Participle[4]		Participle[12]	Participle[6]	Participle[6]	Participle[12]	
m.	παυ-		παυσ-	παυσ-	λαβ-	πε-παυκ-	
f.							
n.							
stem							
	Infinitive[6]		Infinitive[8]	Infinitive[8]	Infinitive[8]	Infinitive[12]	
	παυ-		παυσ-	παυσ-	λαβ-	πε-παυκ-	
	Optative[7]		Optative[12]	Optative[9]	Optative[9]	Optative[15]	
1st s.	παυ-		παυσ-	παυσ-	λαβ-	πε-παυκ-	
2nd s.							
3rd s.							
1st pl.							
2nd pl.							
3rd pl.							
[13] →	Subjunctive ——— →		Subjunctive	Subjunctive	Subjunctive	Subjunctive ———	
1st s.	παυ-		N	παυσ-	λαβ-	πε-παυκ-	
2nd s.			O				
3rd s.			N				
1st pl.			E				
2nd pl.							
3rd pl.							

* only in verbs where the
perfect has a present
meaning (v. rare)

-ά-ομαι PRESENT		-έ-ομαι PRESENT		-ό-ομαι PRESENT	

·DICATIVE (TEMPORAL)

Present[2]	Imperfect[5]	Present[2]	Imperfect[5]	Present *[2]	Imperfect *[5]
'I estimate'	'I was -ing'	'I make'	'I was -ing'	'I am shown'	'I was being -'
τιμ-	ἐ-τιμ-	ποι-	ἐ-ποι	δηλ-	ἐ-δηλ-

·NAUGMENTED FORMS (ASPECTUAL)

Imperative[2]	Imperative[2]	Imperative[2]
τιμ-	ποι-	δηλ-
Participle[4]	**Participle[4]**	**Participle[4]**
τιμ-	ποι-	δηλ-
Infinitive[6]	**Infinitive[6]**	**Infinitive[6]**
τιμ-	ποι-	δηλ-
Optative[7]	**Optative[7]**	**Optative[7]**
τιμ-	ποι-	δηλ-
→ **Subjunctive** ──────→	**Subjunctive** ──────→	**Subjunctive**
τιμ-	ποι-	δηλ-

* δηλό-ομαι is passive in
meaning; but these forms
are the same as the middle

PASSIVE παύ-ομαι 'I am stopped' etc. as MIDDLE: EXCEPT –

IRREGULAR VERBS

	2. FUTURE[11]	3. AORIST[11]
a. INDICATIVE (TEMPORAL)		
	'I shall be stopped'	'I was stopped'
1st s.	παυσθησ-	ἐ-παυσθ-
2nd s.		
3rd s.		
1st pl.		
2nd pl.		
3rd pl.		
b. UNAUGMENTED FORMS (ASPECTUAL)		
	Imperative	Imperative[16]
2nd s.	N	παυσθ-
3rd s.	O	
2nd pl.	N	
3rd pl.	E	
	Participle[12]	Participle[11]
m.	παυσθησ-	παυσθ-
f.		
n.		
stem		
	Infinitive[11]	Infinitive[11]
	παυσθησ-	παυσθ-
	Optative[12]	Optative[12]
1st s.	παυσθησ-	παυσθ-
2nd s.		
3rd s.		
1st pl.		
2nd pl.		
3rd pl.		
[13] → Subjunctive →		Subjunctive →
1st s.	N	παυσθ-
2nd s.	O	
3rd s.	N	
1st pl.	E	
2nd pl.		
3rd pl.		

	εἰμί 'I am' (fut. ἔσ-ομαι*)	
a. INDICATIVE (TEMPORAL)		
	Present[1]	Imperfect[5]
	'I am'	'I was'
1st s.	εἰμί	ἦ
2nd s.		
3rd s.		
1st pl.		
2nd pl.		
3rd pl.		
b. UNAUGMENTED FORMS (A		
	Imperative[8]	
2nd s.	ἴσθι	
3rd s.		
2nd pl.		
3rd pl.		
	Participle[4]	
m.	ὤν	
f.		
n.		
stem		
	Infinitive[6]	
	Optative[11]	
1st s.	εἴ-ην	
2nd s.		
3rd s.		
1st pl.		
2nd pl.		
3rd pl.		
	Subjunctive –	
1st s.	ὦ	
2nd s.		
3rd s.		
1st pl.		
2nd pl.		
3rd pl.		

* 3rd s. ἔσται

-μι¹¹	ἀφ-ίημι¹⁶	δίδω-μι⁹	τίθη-μι¹¹	ἵστη-μι¹¹	ἀφ-ίημι¹⁶
setting up'	'I was sending'	'I gave'	'I placed'	'I set up'	'I sent'
	ἀφ-ίη-ν ἀφ-ιε-	ἐ-δω-κα	ἐ-θη-κα	ἐ-στησ-	ἀφ-ῆ-κα
		ἐ-δο-	ἐ-θε-		ἀφ-ει-

b. UNAUGMENTED FORMS (ASPECTUAL)

		Imperative			
	2nd s.	δο-	θε-	στησ-	ἀφ-ε-
	3rd s.				
	2nd pl.				
njugate like παύσ-ω	3rd pl.				
		Participle			
	m.	δο-	θε-	στησ-	ἀφ-ε-
	f.				
njugate like πέπαυκα	n. stem				
		Infinitive			
		δο-	θε-	στησ-	ἀφ-ε-
		Optative			
	1st s.	δο-	θε-	στησ-	ἀφ-ε-
	2nd s.				
	3rd s.				
	1st pl.				
	2nd pl.				
	3rd pl.				
¹³ ⟶		Subjunctive			⟶ ¹⁶
	1st s.	δ-ῶ	θ-	στησ-	ἀφ-
	2nd s.	δ-ῷς			
	3rd s.				
	1st pl.				
	2nd pl.				
	3rd pl.				

	PRESENT				IMPERFECT	
a. INDICATIVE (TEMPORAL)						
	δίδο-μαι[9]	τίθε-μαι[11]	ἵστα-μαι[11]	ἀφ-ίε-μαι[16]	δίδο-μαι[9]	τίθε-μα
	'I am -ing'	'I am -ing'	'I stand up'	'I am -ing'	'I was -ing'	'I was
1st s.	διδο-	τιθε-	ἱστα-	ἀφ-ιε-	ἐ-δίδο-	ἐ-τιθε-
2nd s.						
3rd s.						
1st pl.						
2nd pl.						
3rd pl.						

b. UNAUGMENTED FORMS (ASPECTUAL)

	Imperative			
2nd s.	δίδο-	τιθε-	ἱστα-	ἀφ-ιε-
3rd s.				
2nd pl.				
3rd pl.				
	Participle			
m.	δίδο-	τιθε-	ἱστα-	ἀφ-ιε-
f.				
n.				
stem				
	Infinitive			
	δίδο-	τιθε-	ἱστα-	ἀφ-ιε-
	Optative			
1st s.	δίδο-	τιθε-	ἱστα-	ἀφ-ιε-
2nd s.				
3rd s.				
1st pl.				
2nd pl.				
3rd pl.				

[13] ⟶	Subjunctive ⟶			[16]
1st s.	διδ-ῶμαι	τιθ-	ἱστ-	ἀφ-ι-
2nd s.	διδ-ῷ			
3rd s.				
1st pl.				
2nd pl.				
3rd pl.				

NOTES

Future: δίδο-μαι
τίθε-μαι
ἵστα-μαι
ἀφ-ίε-μα

* 'I shall s

Perfect: δίδο-μαι
τίθε-μαι
ἵστα-μα
ἀφ-ίε-μα

* 'I stand

Perfe

Passive: Future δ
σ

Aorist ἐ-
ἐ-

Aor.	Perf.	Aor. Pass.

IMPORTANT PRINCIPAL PARTS: 2

Verb	Meaning	Main stem (no aug.)	Fu
λαγχάν-ω			
λαμβάν-ω			
λανθάν-ω			
λέγ-ω			
λείπ-ω			
μανθάν-ω			
μιμνήσκ-ομαι			
οἶδα			
ὄλλυ-μι			
ὁρά-ω			
πάσχ-ω			
πέμπ-ω			
πίν-ω			
πίπτ-ω			
πράττω			
πυνθάν-ομαι			
τίθη-μι			
τίκτ-ω			
τρέπ-ω			
τρέφ-ω			
τρέχ-ω			
τυγχάν-ω			
ὑπισχνέ-ομαι			
φαίν-ω			
φέρ-ω			
φεύγ-ω			
φημί			
φθάν-ω			
φθείρ-ω			
φύ-ω			
ὠνέ-ομαι			

10

	Aor.	Perf.	Aor. Pass.

Verb	Meaning	Main stem (no aug.)	Fut.
ἀγγέλλ-ω			
ἄγ-ω			
αἱρέ-ω			
αἰσθάν-ομαι			
ἀκού-ω			
ἁλίσκ-ομαι			
ἁμαρτάν-ω			
ἄρχ-ω			
βαίν-ω			
βάλλ-ω			
βούλ-ομαι			
γαμέ-ω			
γίγν-ομαι			
γιγνώσκ-ω			
δάκν-ω			
δείκν-υμι			
δίδω-μι			
δύνα-μαι			
εἰμί			
εἶμι			
ἔρχ-ομαι			
ἐρωτά-ω			
ἐσθί-ω			
εὑρίσκ-ω			
ἔχ-ω			
-θνήσκ-ω			
ἵη-μι			
ἱκνέ-ομαι			
ἵστη-μι			
καλέ-ω			
κεῖ-μαι			
κόπτ-ω			
κτείν-ω			

AORIST MIDDLE

ἵστα-μαι[11]	ἀφ-ίε-μαι[16]	δίδο-μαι[9]	τίθε-μαι[11]	ἵστα-μαι[11]	ἀφ-ίε-μαι[16]
'I was -ing up'	'I was -ing'	'I -ed'	'I -ed'	'I stood up'	'I -ed'
ἱστα-	ἀφ-ιε-	ἐ-δο-	ἐ-θε-	ἔ-στ-ην	ἀφ-ει-

b. UNAUGMENTED FORMS (ASPECTUAL)

	Imperative			
2nd s.	δο-	θοῦ	στη-	ἀφ-οῦ
3rd s.		θε-		ἀφ-ε-
2nd pl.				
3rd pl.			στα-	
	Participle			
m.	δο-	θε-	στα-	ἀφ-ε-
f.				
n.				
stem				
	Infinitive			
	δο-	θε-	στη-	ἀφ-ε-
	Optative			
1st s.	δο-	θε-	στα-	ἀφ-ε-
2nd s.				
3rd s.				
1st pl.				
2nd pl.				
3rd pl.				
[13] → Subjunctive				→ 16
1st s.	δ-ῶμαι	θ-	στ-	ἀφ-
2nd s.	δ-ῷ			
3rd s.				
1st pl.				
2nd pl.				
3rd pl.				

Left-margin notes:

-ομαι
ομαι
-ομαι* } like παύσ-ομαι
σ-ομαι

ο-μαι } like λέλυμαι
ε-μαι
κ-α* — like λέλυκα
-ιμαι — like λέλυμαι

ἔστα-θι
ἐστ-ώς (or ἐστηκώς)
ἐστά-ναι
ἐστα-ίην
ἐστ-ῶ
e ἔστα-μαι

ι, τεθήσ-ομαι,
αι, ἀφ-εθήσ-ομαι
ἐ-τέθ-ην,
ἀφ-είθ-ην

-μι VERBS – ACTIVE

	PRESENT				IMPERFECT	
a. INDICATIVE (TEMPORAL)				INDICATIVE		
	δίδω-μι[9]	τίθη-μι[11]	ἵστη-μι[11]	ἀφ-ίη-μι[16]	δίδω-μι[9]	τίθη-μι[11]
	'I give'	'I place'	'I set up'	'I send'	'I was giving'	'I was placing'
1st s.	διδω-	τιθη-	ἱστη-	ἀφ-ιη-	ἐ-διδο-	ἐ-τιθη-
2nd s.						ἐ-τιθε-
3rd s.						
1st pl.	διδο-	τιθε-	ἱστα-	ἀφ-ιε-		
2nd pl.						
3rd pl.				ἀφ-ι-		

b. UNAUGMENTED FORMS (ASPECTUAL)

Imperative				
2nd s.	διδο-	τιθε-	ἱστη	ἀφ-ιε-
3rd s.			ἱστα-	
2nd pl.				
3rd pl.				
Participle				
m.	διδο-	τιθε-	ἱστα-	ἀφ-ιε-
f.				
n.				
stem				
Infinitive				
	διδο-	τιθε-	ιστα-	ἀφ-ιε-
Optative				
1st s.	διδο-	τιθε-	ιστα-	ἀφ-ιε-
2nd s.				
3rd s.				
1st pl.				
2nd pl.				
3rd pl.				
13 → **Subjunctive** → 16				
1st s.	διδ-ῶ	τιθ-	ιστ-	ἀφ-ι-
2nd s.	διδ-ῷς			
3rd s.				
1st pl.				
2nd pl.				
3rd pl.				

NOTES

Future:
δίδω-μι	δώσ-ω
τίθη-μι	θήσ-ω
ἵστη-μι	στήσ-ω
ἵη-μι	ἥσ-ω

Perfect:
δίδω-μι	δέ-δω
τίθη-μι	τέ-θηκ
ἵστη-μι	see Mi
ἵη-μι	εἷκ-α

'I know' (fut. εἴσ-ομαι)		εἶμι 'I shall go'		φημί 'I say' (fut. φήσ-ω)	
nt[1]	Imperfect[6]	Future[5]	Imperfect[6]	Present[6]	Imperfect[6]
w'	'I knew'	'I shall go'	'I went'	'I say'	'I said'
	ᾔδ-η	εἶμι	ᾔ-α	φημί	ἔ-φ-ην

UAL)

rative[8]		Imperative 'go!'[8]		Imperative[16]	
		ἴθι		φάθι	
ciple[6]		Participle 'going'[7]		Participle[8]	
ς		ἰών		φάς	
itive[6]		Infinitive 'to go'[6]		Infinitive[11]	
tive[11]		Optative[11]		Optative[8]	
-ην		ἴ-οιμι		φαί-ην	
unctive ──────▶		Subjunctive ──────▶		Subjunctive	
ῶ		ἴ-ω		φ-ῶ	

MIDDLE παύ-ομαι *'I cease, stop'* (with strong aorist of λαμβάν-ομαι)

	1. PRESENT		2.FUTURE	3. AORIST		4. PERFECT	
a. INDICATIVE (TEMPORAL)							
	Present[2]	Imperfect[5]	Future[5]	Weak[5]	Strong[5]	Perfect[12]	Pluperfect[15]
	'I stop'	*'I was -ing'*	*'I shall -'*	*'I stopped'*	*'I took'*	*'I have -ed'*	*'I had -ed'*
1st s.	παυ-	ἐ-παυ-	παυσ-	ἐ-παυσ-	ἐ-λαβ-	πε-παυ-	ἐ-πε-παυ-
2nd s.							
3rd s.							
1st pl.							
2nd pl.							
3rd pl.							
b. UNAUGMENTED FORMS (ASPECTUAL)							
	Imperative[2/8]		Imperative	Imperative[8]	Imperative[8]	Imperative	
2nd s.	παυ-		N	παυσ-	λαβ-	πέ-παυ-σο	
3rd s.			O			-σθω	
2nd pl.			N			-σθε	
3rd pl.			E			-σθων	
	Participle[4]		Participle[12]	Participle[6]	Participle[6]	Participle[12]	
m.	παυ-		παυσ-	παυσ-	λαβ-	πε-παυ-	
f.							
n.							
stem							
	Infinitive[6]		Infinitive[8]	Infinitive[8]	Infinitive[8]	Infinitive[12]	
	παυ-		παυσ-	παυσ-	λαβ-·	πε-παυ-	
	Optative[7]		Optative[12]	Optative[9]	Optative[9]	Optative[15]	
1st s.	παυ-		παυσ-	παυσ-	λαβ-	πε-παυ-	
2nd s.							
3rd s.							
1st pl.							
2nd pl.							
3rd pl.							
[13] ⟶	Subjunctive ⟶		Subjunctive	Subjunctive	Subjunctive	Subjunctive ⟶	
1st s.	παυ-		N	παυσ-	λαβ-	πε-παυ-	
2nd s.			O				
3rd s.			N				
1st pl.			E				
2nd pl.							
3rd pl.							

5

	-ά-ω PRESENT		-έ-ω PRESENT		-ό-ω PRESENT	
a. INDICATIVE (TEMPORAL)						
	Present	*Imperfect*	*Present*	*Imperfect*	*Present*	*Imperfect*
	'I honour'[1]	'I was -ing'[5]	'I do'[1]	'I was doing'[5]	'I show'[2]	'I was -ing'[5]
1st s.	τιμ-	ἐ-τιμ-	ποι-	ἐ-ποι-	δηλ-	ἐ-δηλ-
2nd s.						
3rd s.						
1st pl.						
2nd pl.						
3rd pl.						

b. UNAUGMENTED FORMS (ASPECTUAL)

	Imperative[1]	Imperative[1]	Imperative[2]
2nd s.	τιμ-	ποι-	δηλ-
3rd s.			
2nd pl.			
3rd pl.			
	Participle[4]	Participle[4]	Participle[4]
m.	τιμ-	ποι-	δηλ-
f.			
n.			
stem			
	Infinitive[6]	Infinitive[6]	Infinitive[6]
	τιμ-	ποι-	δηλ-
	Optative[7]	Optative[7]	Optative[7]
1st s.	τιμ-	ποι-	δηλ
2nd s.			
3rd s.			
1st pl.			
2nd pl.			
3rd pl.			
→	Subjunctive ———→	Subjunctive ———→	Subjunctive
1st s.	τιμ-	ποι-	δηλ-
2nd s.			
3rd s.			
1st pl.			
2nd pl.			
3rd pl.			

IRREGULAR

		singular					plural			
		nom.	stem	acc.	gen.⁷	dat.⁸	nom.	acc.	gen.⁷	dat.⁸
noun irr.	f.	ναῦς	(ναυ-)	3			3			
noun irr.	m.	Ζεύς	(Δι-)	3						

MIXED ADJECTIVES – FIRST AND THIRD DECLENSION

PRONOUNS

	singular				plural			
	nom.	acc.	gen.⁷	dat.⁸	nom.	acc.	gen.⁷	dat.⁸
ἐγώ	3				ἡμεῖς	3		
σύ	3				ὑμεῖς	3		

		singular					plural			
		nom.	stem	acc.	gen.⁷	dat.⁸	nom.	acc.	gen.⁷	dat.⁸
m.	γλυκύς*	(γλυκ-(ε)-)		9						
f.	γλυκεῖα	(γλυκει-)		9						
n.	γλυκύ	(γλυκ-(ε)-)		9						

* *Comparative* γλυκ-ύτερ-ος   *Superlative* γλυκ-ύτατ-ος

OTHER MIXED ADJECTIVES – NOTES

Participles in -ων -ουσα -ον *(stem -οντ-)* ⎫
Participles in -ας -ασα -αν *(stem -αντ-)* ⎬ m./n. endings like εὔφρων   f. endings like τόλμα
Participles in -εις -εισα -εν *(stem -εντ-)* ⎭

Participles in -ως -υια -ος *(stem -οτ-)*   m./n. endings like εὔφρων   f. endings like ἡμετέρα

οὐδείς οὐδεμία οὐδέν *(stem οὐδεν-)*   m./n. endings like εὔφρων   f. endings like ἡμετέρα

| plural | | | | | NEUTER singular | | |
nom.[2]	acc.[2]	gen.[7]	dat.[8]		nom.[1]	acc.[1]	gen.[7]
				def. art.			
				2b noun ἔργ-ον			
				καλ-όν			
				ἡμέτερ-ον		like καλ-όν	

| plural | | | | NEUTER singular | |
nom.[3]	acc.[3]	gen.[7]	dat.[8]	nom.[3]	acc.[3]
μεγαλ-				μεγ-	μεγ-
πολλ-				πολ-	πολ-
αὐτ-	ταυτ-	τουτ-	ταυτ-	τουτ-	τουτ-

COMPARISON OF ADVERBS

REGULAR			IRREGULAR	
			Adjective	Adverb
Positive:	-ως		ἀγαθ-ός	
Comparative:	-ο } -ω } τερ-ον		μέγας	
			πολύς	
Superlative:	-ο } -ω } τατ-α			

	MASCULINE				plu
	singular				
	nom.[1]	acc.[1]	gen.[7]	dat.[8]	nor
def. art.					
2a noun ἄνθρωπ-ος					
adjective καλ-ός					
ἡμέτερ-ος			like καλ-ός		

IRREGULAR ADJECTIVES

MASCULINE					
singular				plural	
nom.[3]	acc.[3]	gen.[7]	dat.[8]	nom.[3]	acc.[3]
μεγ-	μεγ-	μεγαλ-		μεγαλ-	
πολ-	πολ-	πολλ-		πολλ-	
οὗτ-	τουτ-	τουτ-	τουτ-	οὗτ-	τουτ-

COMPARISON OF AD

REGULAR

Comparatives: -o } τερ-ος
-ω

like ἡμέτερ-

Superlatives: -o } τατ-ος
-ω

like καλ-ός

PUBLISHED BY THE PRESS SYNDICATE OF THE UNIVERSITY OF CAMBRIDGE
The Pitt Building, Trumpington Street, Cambridge, United Kingdom

CAMBRIDGE UNIVERSITY PRESS
The Edinburgh Building, Cambridge CB2 2RU, UK
40 West 20th Street, New York, NY 10011-4211, USA
477 Williamstown Road, Port Melbourne, VIC 3207, Australia
Ruiz de Alarcón 13, 28014 Madrid, Spain
Dock House, The Waterfront, Cape Town 8001, South Africa

http://www.cambridge.org

First published 1978
Ninth printing 2003

Printed in the United Kingdom by Cambridge Printing, the printing business of
Cambridge University Press

ISBN 0 521 22052 1

ISBN 0-521-22052-1

9 780521 220521